Greetings From AMERICA

Postcards from Donovan and Daisy

U.S. GEOGRAPHY
FLYING RHINOCEROS

RAY NELSON
AND
DOUGLAS KELLY

Scholastic Inc.

New York   Toronto   London   Auckland   Sydney

To Theresa and Victoria

ISBN 0-590-97438-6

12 11 10 9 8 7 6 5 4 3 2 1   6 7 8 9/9 0 1/0

Printed in the U.S.A.   09

First Scholastic printing, September 1996

INTRODUCTION

Like Donovan and Daisy in this story, I once spent a lot of time "chasing a ball" across America. Before I was a United States senator, I played basketball for ten years with the New York Knicks. As we traveled from state to state and game to game, I learned about our country and made many good friends along the way.

As a senator, I still enjoy learning about different people and places, and I want all children to have that opportunity. Several years ago, to help encourage more kids to study geography, I initiated a program called Geography Awareness Week. I also sponsored a quiz on geography that started in my state of New Jersey and has since developed into the annual National Geography Bee.

I'm sure you'll enjoy reading *Greetings from America*. When you have finished chasing the red ball, I hope that Donovan and Daisy's travels will inspire you to embark on your own journey of learning and discovery about our country and our world.

Bill Bradley

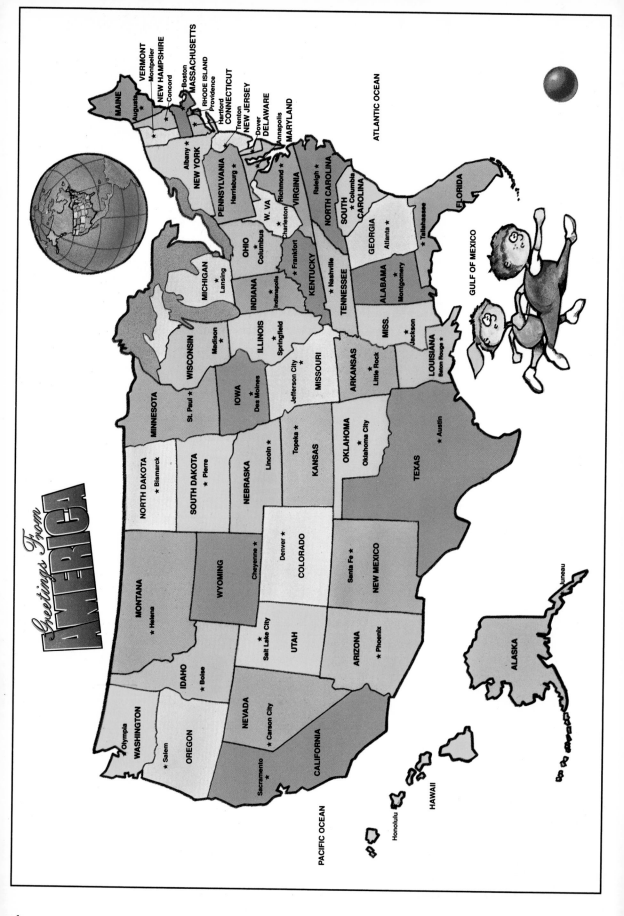

Greetings From AMERICA

PACIFIC OCEAN

WASHINGTON
★ Olympia

OREGON
★ Salem

NEVADA
★ Carson City

CALIFORNIA
★ Sacramento

IDAHO
★ Boise

UTAH
★ Salt Lake City

ARIZONA
★ Phoenix

MONTANA
★ Helena

WYOMING
★ Cheyenne

COLORADO
Denver ★

NEW MEXICO
Santa Fe ★

NORTH DAKOTA
★ Bismarck

SOUTH DAKOTA
★ Pierre

NEBRASKA
Lincoln ★

KANSAS
Topeka ★

OKLAHOMA
★ Oklahoma City

TEXAS
★ Austin

MINNESOTA
St. Paul ★

IOWA
Des Moines ★

MISSOURI
Jefferson City ★

ARKANSAS
Little Rock ★

LOUISIANA
Baton Rouge ★

WISCONSIN
Madison ★

MICHIGAN
Lansing ★

ILLINOIS
Springfield ★

INDIANA
Indianapolis ★

OHIO
Columbus ★

KENTUCKY
Frankfort ★

TENNESSEE
★ Nashville

MISS.
Jackson ★

ALABAMA
Montgomery ★

GEORGIA
Atlanta ★

FLORIDA
Tallahassee ★

W. VA
Charleston ★

VIRGINIA
Richmond ★

NORTH CAROLINA
Raleigh ★

SOUTH CAROLINA
Columbia ★

PENNSYLVANIA
Harrisburg ★

NEW YORK
Albany ★

MAINE
Augusta ★

VERMONT
Montpelier ★

NEW HAMPSHIRE
Concord ★

MASSACHUSETTS
Boston ★

RHODE ISLAND
Providence ★

CONNECTICUT
Hartford ★

NEW JERSEY
Trenton ★

DELAWARE
Dover ★

MARYLAND
Annapolis ★

ATLANTIC OCEAN

GULF OF MEXICO

ALASKA
Juneau ★

HAWAII
Honolulu ★

4

It was a beautiful day, sometime last fall,
when Donovan and Daisy went out to play ball.
OOOOPS!
Donovan threw it too fast and too high.
It sailed over Daisy, up into the sky.
"We'll catch the ball, Dexter, it shouldn't be hard—
if it takes very long, we'll drop you a card."

WESTERN MEADOWLARK

POST CARD

Dear Dexter,

   Well, we're on our way! We left Oregon today chasing after that crazy red ball.

   So far we've seen beaches, deserts, beautiful valleys, and mountains.

   Oregon's economy depends on forestry, as well as tourism and farming.

   See you soon!

Donovan and Daisy

State Capital: Salem

Dexter Willoughby
P.O. Box 19894
Portland, OR
97219

GREETINGS FROM **OREGON**

OREGON GRAPE

The ball got away, rolling down a big hill.
It bounced off a beaver and caused quite a spill.
There in a tangle were bird, fish and beast,
but the ball squirted free and headed due east.

6

Greetings FROM

Dear Dexter,
   Here we are in Idaho. Many people visit this state to go camping and river rafting. We chased the ball through Sun Valley, which is famous for its skiing and swimming.
   What we can't figure out is how Idaho got its name. No one seems to know.
   We're missing you tons!
      Donovan

SYRINGA

State Capital: Boise

POST CARD

Dexter Willoughby
P.O. Box 19894
Portland, OR
97219

MOUNTAIN BLUEBIRD

It crashed into a truck just outside of Boise,
causing a ruckus and becoming quite noisy.
Now out of control, the truck dumped its load,
and a shipment of spuds spilled onto the road.

WASHINGTON

RHODODENDRON

SEATTLE

Dear Dexter,

We're writing this postcard from the top of the Space Needle. The Space Needle is a very tall tower that overlooks Seattle. Washington has wilderness areas full of steelhead trout, western hemlock trees, and rhodo-dendrons. Lumber, apples, blueberries, hops, and red raspberries are just a few of the crops that Washington produces.

Still no sign of the ball... see you soon!

Donovan

POST CARD

Dexter Willoughby
P.O. Box 19894
Portland, OR
97219

State Capital: Olympia

WILLOW GOLDFINCH

A sight then appeared that was really absurd:
the ball was picked up by a very small bird.
Way over Seattle he caught a good breeze,
that carried him high to the tops of the trees.
The goldfinch grew tired of the ball in his home,
so he kicked it—real hard—in the direction of Nome.

ALASKA

POST CARD

Dear Dexter,
  We hope everything at home is okay.
  We're writing from Alaska, which is the biggest state in America. In case you are wondering, Alaska got its name from an Eskimo word meaning "Great Land," or "That which the sea breaks against."

We really like playing in the snow, but we miss you!
  Hope to see you soon!

love, Donovan

State Capital: Juneau

FORGET-ME-NOT

WILLOW PTARMIGAN

**Some Eskimos watched as it shot in the air,
and bounced off the head of a big polar bear.
Over the tundra and into the bay,
it caught in a current and sailed far away.**

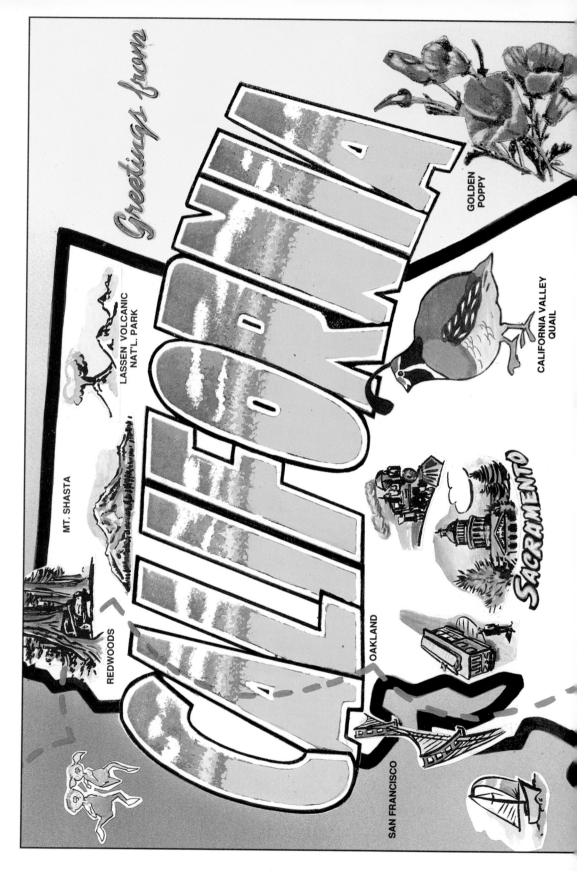

The ball bobbed beneath the Golden Gate Bridge,
rolled up to the beach and over a ridge,

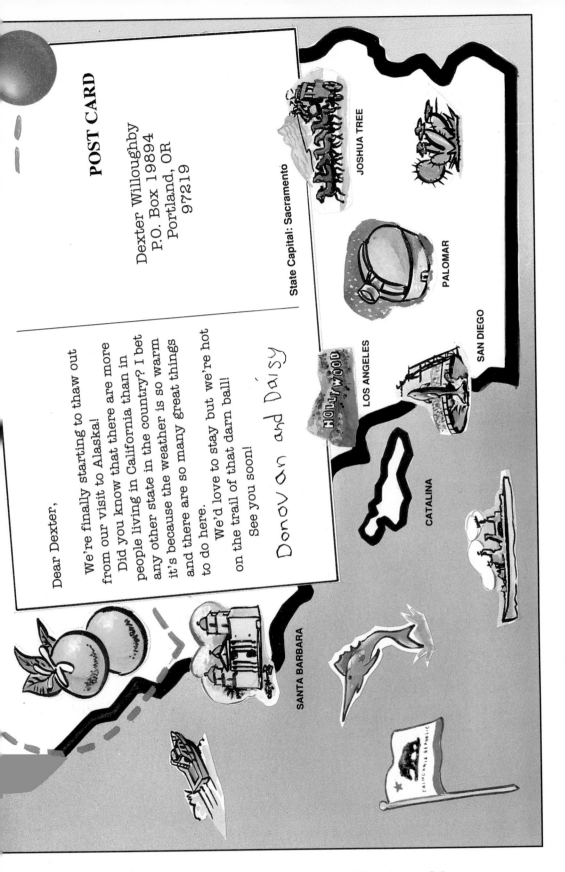

POST CARD

Dexter Willoughby
P.O. Box 19894
Portland, OR
97219

State Capital: Sacramento

JOSHUA TREE

PALOMAR

SAN DIEGO

LOS ANGELES

HOLLYWOOD

CATALINA

SANTA BARBARA

CALIFORNIA REPUBLIC

Dear Dexter,

We're finally starting to thaw out from our visit to Alaska! Did you know that there are more people living in California than in any other state in the country? I bet it's because the weather is so warm and there are so many great things to do here.

We'd love to stay but we're hot on the trail of that darn ball!

See you soon!

Donovan and Daisy

by orange groves and freeways flowing with cars.
The kids stopped to chat with a few movie stars.

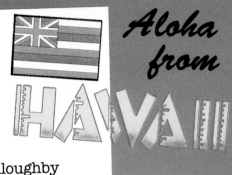

Aloha from
HAWAII

Aloha from Hawaii, Dexter!

Did you know that there are eight main islands in this state? The islands are Hawaii, Kahoolawe, Maui, Lanai, Molokai, Oahu, Kauai, and Niihau. The weather in Hawaii is beautiful. The soil is perfect for growing tropical fruits and vegetables.

Time to go! We've got to get our grass skirts on so we can go to our hula lessons.

love, Donovan

Dexter Willoughby
P.O. Box 19894
Portland, OR
97219

State Capital: Honolulu

NENE
(HAWAIIAN GOOSE)

HIBISCUS

The ball rolled with the motion of a shiny blue ocean
as the boy and the girl gave chase.
It surfed on the sea near a purple palm tree,
and vanished with hardly a trace.

Dear Dexter,
Oregon may be known for all its rain, but Nevada is definitely the driest state we've seen! What's even funnier is that the name Nevada comes from a Spanish word meaning "snowcapped." The state has an overall average rainfall of only 7 inches per year.
Utah was named for a word meaning "people of the mountains." They mine copper, gold, silver, lead, and zinc here.

NEVADA

Dexter Willoughby
P.O. Box 19894
Portland, OR
97219

State Capital: Carson City, Nevada
State Capital: Salt Lake City, Utah

SAGEBRUSH

BLUEBIRD

SEAGULL

SEGO LILY

UTAH

**Running down the Vegas strip,
they didn't get a break,
by Carson City, Winnemucca,
then the Great Salt Lake.**

Dear Dexter,

We saw some really cool things in Arizona. We visited the Grand Canyon, the Petrified Forest, Hoover Dam, Lake Mead, Fort Apache, and the Painted Desert.

Daisy and I bought you a bolo tie, which is the official state neckwear of Arizona. The name Arizona is from the Indian word "Arizonac," meaning "little spring."

POST CARD

Dexter Willoughby
P.O. Box 19894
Portland, OR
97219

State Capital: Phoenix

SAGUARO

CACTUS WREN

ARIZONA

**They entered a land that was covered by sand,
with cactus that grew rather tall.**

Dear Dexter,

How are things back home? We've been riding donkeys across the state of New Mexico all day looking for that silly ball.

This state is mostly desert, but there are a lot of farms around Albuquerque and Santa Fe. These farms grow all kinds of cereals, fruits, and vegetables (the official state vegetables, by the way, are chiles and frijoles).

Donovan

POST CARD

State Capital: Santa Fe

YUCCA

ROADRUNNER

They soaked in the sights under Santa Fe's lights, on a donkey that moved at a crawl.

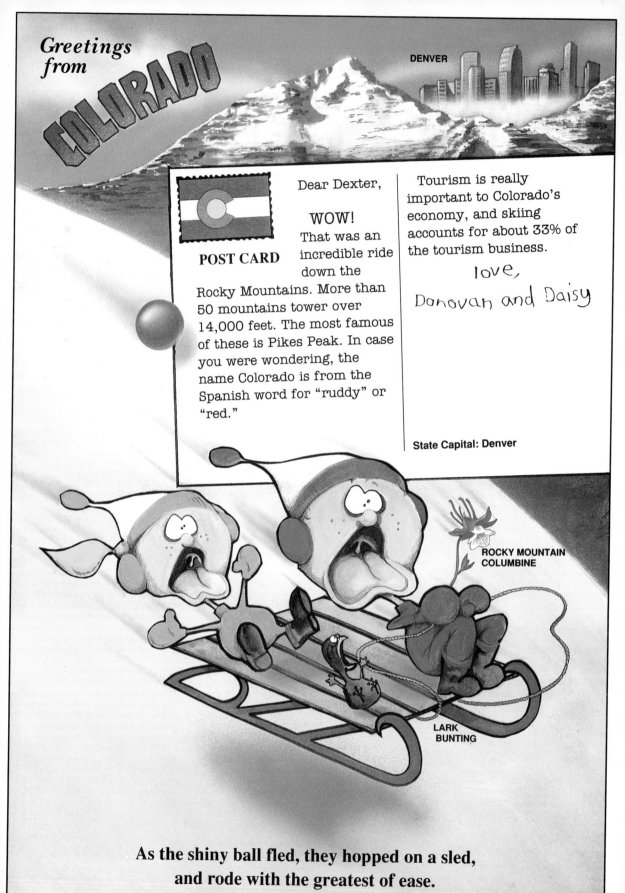

Greetings from COLORADO

DENVER

Dear Dexter,

WOW!
That was an incredible ride down the Rocky Mountains. More than 50 mountains tower over 14,000 feet. The most famous of these is Pikes Peak. In case you were wondering, the name Colorado is from the Spanish word for "ruddy" or "red."

POST CARD

Tourism is really important to Colorado's economy, and skiing accounts for about 33% of the tourism business.

love,
Donovan and Daisy

State Capital: Denver

ROCKY MOUNTAIN COLUMBINE

LARK BUNTING

**As the shiny ball fled, they hopped on a sled,
and rode with the greatest of ease.**

WYOMING

MEADOWLARK

INDIAN PAINTBRUSH

MONTANA

WESTERN MEADOWLARK

BITTER-ROOT

MONTANA

Dear Dexter,

Boy, are we pooped! We just spent the entire day chasing the ball across Montana and Wyoming. Montana got its name from a Latin word meaning "mountainous."

Wyoming was the first state in the nation to give women the right to vote. It also had the first woman governor, Mrs. Nellie Taylor Ross, in 1925. We almost caught the ball in Casper, so it shouldn't be long now!

Donovan

WYOMING

Dexter Willoughby
P.O. Box 19894
Portland, OR
97219

State Capital: Cheyenne, Wyoming
State Capital: Helena, Montana

They followed a route that took them through Butte, and then to a sheep wearing skis.

Dear Dexter,

We're writing to you from a cornfield in Nebraska! Nebraska, which is from an Oto Indian word meaning "flat water," was part of the Louisiana Purchase in 1803. Nebraska is known for its agriculture. Farms produce large amounts of corn, rye, wheat, cattle, and hogs. We met some really nice pigs; I think you would like them.

Donovan and Daisy

Dexter Willoughby
P.O. Box 19894
Portland, OR
97219

State Capital: Lincoln

WESTERN MEADOWLARK

GOLDENROD

NEBRASKA

**The kids could have sworn, as they entered the corn,
that the chase was close to complete.**

18

Dear Dexter,
We are standing in the exact center of the United States of America. There are rolling plains of wheat as far as the eye can see. Kansas got its name from a Siouan word meaning "people of the south wind."

Well, we have to go. A farmer just told us the ball bounced by his combine this morning and if we hurry we might catch it.

Donavan

SUNFLOWER

Greetings From

KANSAS

Dexter Willoughby
P.O. Box 19894
Portland, OR
97219

State Capital: Topeka

WESTERN MEADOWLARK

It's not easy to say how the ball slipped away,
but it vanished in a field full of wheat.

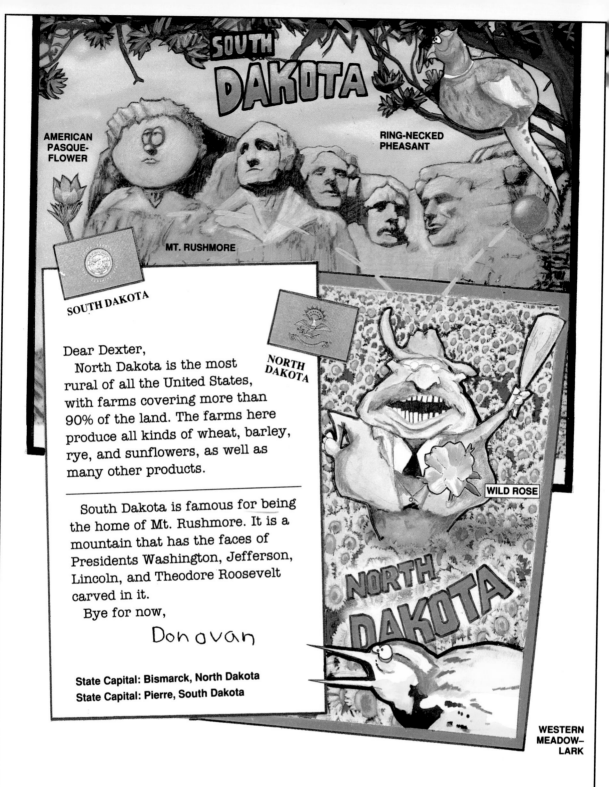

SOUTH DAKOTA

AMERICAN PASQUE-FLOWER

RING-NECKED PHEASANT

MT. RUSHMORE

SOUTH DAKOTA

NORTH DAKOTA

WILD ROSE

NORTH DAKOTA

WESTERN MEADOW-LARK

Dear Dexter,

North Dakota is the most rural of all the United States, with farms covering more than 90% of the land. The farms here produce all kinds of wheat, barley, rye, and sunflowers, as well as many other products.

South Dakota is famous for being the home of Mt. Rushmore. It is a mountain that has the faces of Presidents Washington, Jefferson, Lincoln, and Theodore Roosevelt carved in it.

Bye for now,

Donovan

State Capital: Bismarck, North Dakota
State Capital: Pierre, South Dakota

In the strangest of places, watched by presidents' faces,
the ball next came into view.
Over water, then air, and the streets of Pierre,
there goes the ball . . . toodle-oo!

SCISSOR-TAILED FLYCATCHER

OKLAHOMA

IS O.K.

OKLAHOMA CITY

REDBUD (STATE TREE)

Dear Dexter,

We almost caught up with the ball here in Oklahoma City, but the winds came up and swept it away.

In 1889, when homesteading was first permitted in Oklahoma, 50,000 people came to the area to get land. The ones who tried to beat the noon starting time were called "sooners" and gave Oklahoma its nickname of the "Sooner State." The state reptile is the mountain boomer lizard.

These lizards are super cool, but Daisy won't let me bring one home.

POST CARD

love,
Donavan and Daisy

State Capital: Oklahoma City

They ran for a spell to a large oil well, where the ball was nestled up high.
Oil started to gush, shooting up with a rush,
and launching the ball to the sky.

It orbited Earth, way over Fort Worth,
crashing down in the Lone Star State.

Howdy pardner!
Texas is huge. It's actually the second largest state in America. There is a bunch of great stuff to see here. We've been to the Alamo, which was a famous fortress during the Mexican-American War of 1836. We also visited the Johnson Space Center in Houston.
Texas gets its name from an Indian word meaning "friends." I got a new cowboy hat. It's really big and covers my eyes. We'll bring one back for you.

love, Donovan

POST CARD

Dexter Willoughby
P.O. Box 19894
Portland, OR
97219

State Capital: Austin

AUSTIN

NASA

THE ALAMO

**By steers that were grazing, it's really amazing,
that the ball didn't pop and deflate.**

MAGNOLIA

LOUISIANA

LOUISIANA

PELICAN

Dear Dexter,
Hope everything is great at home!
Today we chased the ball through Arkansas and Louisiana. Arkansas is the home of the only active diamond mine in America. The mine is a big tourist attraction near Murfreesboro. We dug for awhile but didn't have any luck.
Did you know that Louisiana was named in honor of King Louis XIV of France? We've been to the French Quarter in New Orleans, the Superdome, and Chalmette National Historical Park.
Bye for now.

Donovan and Daisy

State Capital: Baton Rouge, Louisiana
State Capital: Little Rock, Arkansas

ARKANSAS

APPLE BLOSSOM

MOCKINGBIRD

ARKANSAS STATE FLAG

**Down the street and around the block,
they lost the ball in Little Rock.
From bad to worse in Arkansas,
their luck then changed at Mardi Gras.**

GATEWAY ARCH

PONY EXPRESS

JEFFERSON CITY

LAKE TANEYCOMO

MISSOURI

HAWTHORN

BLUEBIRD

Dear Dexter,

Greetings from Missouri. Boy, is there ever a lot to see in this state.

Independence was the starting point in the East for the Pony Express, the Santa Fe Trail, and the Oregon Trail. Missouri has 11 major lakes, Mark Twain's boyhood home, and the house where the famous outlaw Jesse James was killed.

POST CARD

It's named after the Missouri Indian tribe. Missouri means "town of the large canoes."

love,
Donovan and Daisy

State Capital: Jefferson City

Into St. Louis they continued their march,
and chased the ball under the tall Gateway Arch.
The ball left Missouri with hardly a clue,
so the kids paddled north in a big red canoe.

IOWA

EASTERN GOLDFINCH

WILD ROSE

Dear Dexter,
   We've chased the ball all the way into Iowa. The "Hawkeye State" is covered with thousands of farms. They raise oats, soybeans, corn, pigs, sheep, and cows here.
   Iowa gets its name from an Indian word meaning "the beautiful land." We learned that Grant Wood, the artist, was from Iowa. He painted that famous picture, *American Gothic.*

   Take care of yourself...we'll see you soon.

love,

Donovan

State Capital: Des Moines

**They followed the ball just as fast as they could,
past a famous old painting by a man named Grant Wood.**

WISCONSIN

SWISS

ROBIN

WOOD VIOLET

BADGER

CHEDDAR

JACK

Greetings from

MINNESOTA

LOON

MINNESOTA

ST. PAUL

PINK & WHITE LADY'S SLIPPER

WISCONSIN

Dear Dexter,
    Well, we almost caught up with the ball in St. Paul, Minnesota, but lost it again when we crossed into Wisconsin. The name Minnesota comes from a Dakota Indian word meaning "sky-tinted water."
    Wisconsin has more milk cows than any other state. The state produces about 17% of the nation's

milk, and also is the biggest producer of cheese in the country.
    I wish we could bring back a big bowl of fresh milk for you! Hope to see you soon!

love,
Donovan and Daisy

State Capital: Madison, Wisconsin
State Capital: St. Paul, Minnesota

They chased the ball near St. Paul,
they thought they couldn't miss.
It bounced about the dairy cows,
by Cheddar, Jack, and Swiss.

ILLINOIS

Dear Dexter,
Here we are in the heartland of America! Illinois grows and ships more agricultural products than any other state. We've seen many memorials to Abraham Lincoln in central Illinois. The Lincoln Home, the Lincoln Tomb, and the restored Old State Capitol are all located in Springfield.

We visited Indiana, which means "land of Indians." The state is a national leader in farming. Corn, soy beans, hogs, wheat, and oats are some of the crops grown in Indiana.

Donovan and Daisy

State Capital: Indianapolis, Indiana
State Capital: Springfield, Illinois

VISIT
ILLINOIS

SPRINGFIELD

CARDINAL   VIOLET

HEART
OF
LINCOLN LAND

INDIANA

PEONY

CARDINAL

**They zipped through Chicago,
where their great hectic chase suddenly turned into an all out race!
The kids rushed around, both near and far,
as they followed the ball in a fast Indy car!!**

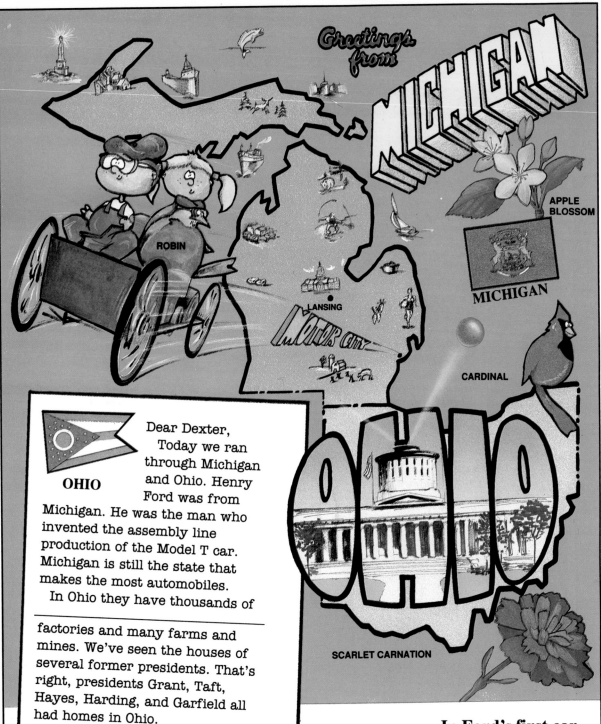

Greetings from MICHIGAN

ROBIN

APPLE BLOSSOM

MICHIGAN

LANSING

MOTOR CITY

CARDINAL

OHIO

Dear Dexter,
   Today we ran through Michigan and Ohio. Henry Ford was from Michigan. He was the man who invented the assembly line production of the Model T car. Michigan is still the state that makes the most automobiles.
   In Ohio they have thousands of factories and many farms and mines. We've seen the houses of several former presidents. That's right, presidents Grant, Taft, Hayes, Harding, and Garfield all had homes in Ohio.

Donovan and Daisy

State Capital: Lansing, Michigan
State Capital: Columbus, Ohio

SCARLET CARNATION

In Ford's first car
they traveled through Flint,
with no sign of the ball,
not even a hint.
In Cleveland and Canton
they caused quite a stir—
leaving Ohio, the ball was a blur.

Dear Dexter,
    It's amazing how fast these horses run! We are writing from Churchill Downs in Louisville—home of the Kentucky Derby, one of the most famous horse races in the world.
    One of the horses was kind enough to teach us that Kentucky's name is from the Iroquoian word "Ken-tah-ten," meaning "land of tomorrow."
    Bye for now . . .
        Donovan

POST CARD

Dexter Willoughby
P.O. Box 19894
Portland, OR
97219

State Capital: Frankfort

They hopped on a horse, a magnificent steed,
and then out of the gate they flew with great speed.
Around the last corner, down the back stretch she goes!
But the kids miss again . . . the ball wins by a nose.

Dear Dexter,
We are in Nashville, the birthplace of country music and the state capital of Tennessee. Elvis, the King of rock 'n' roll, made Tennessee his home when he built Graceland.

We learned that Alabama produces chemicals, textiles, rubber, and plastics. People here think the name Alabama may have come from a Choctaw Indian word meaning "thicket clearers" or "vegetation gatherers."

love,
Donovan and Daisy

State Capital: Nashville, Tennessee
State Capital: Montgomery, Alabama

SHAKE, RATTLE & ROLL FROM

IRIS

TENNESSEE

MOCKINGBIRD

YELLOWHAMMER

ALABAMA

CAMELLIA

ALABAMA
STATE FLAG

**At Graceland's gates they saw the King,
and stopped a while to hear him sing.
They couldn't stay, they had to scram,
to chase the ball through Birmingham.**

MISSISSIPPI

MAGNOLIA

MOCKINGBIRD

Dear Dexter,
Here we are floating down the big Mississippi River, kind of like Mark Twain's characters Tom Sawyer and Huckleberry Finn. Mississippi comes from an Indian word meaning "Father of Waters."

For well over one hundred years, cotton was Mississippi's major crop. The state now depends on its soybean crop for a big part of its economy. Mississippi is the world's largest producer of pond-raised catfish. We'll try to bring you one for supper, Dexter!

Donovan and Daisy

State Capital: Jackson

**On the Mississippi the ball began to float,
caught up in the paddle of a big riverboat.**

Greetings from **GEORGIA**

CHEROKEE ROSE

BROWN THRASHER

TALLAHASSEE

JACKSONVILLE

ORANGE BLOSSOM

Greetings from **Florida**

FLORIDA

GEORGIA

TAMPA

MIAMI

MOCKINGBIRD

Dear Dexter,
Boy, is it warm here in Florida.

Millions of tourists from all over the world come here every year. They come to see Miami Beach, NASA's Kennedy Space Center, Everglades National Park, and the Epcot Center. Florida is from the Spanish, meaning "feast of flowers."

We also spent some time in Georgia. Did you know Georgia grows twice as many peanuts as the next leading state?

Daisy just tried eating a peach and peanut butter sandwich...ugh!

love,
Donovan and Daisy

State Capital: Atlanta, Georgia
State Capital: Tallahassee, Florida

Through cotton fields and everglades the ball then headed south,
bouncing high and bouncing low, across a gator's mouth.

Greetings from **NORTH CAROLINA**

CARDINAL

DOGWOOD

NORTH CAROLINA

Greetings from **SOUTH CAROLINA**

CAROLINA YELLOW JESSAMINE

CAROLINA WREN

SOUTH CAROLINA

Dear Dexter,
    North Carolina is the nation's biggest producer of brick, furniture, and textiles. The state also has a large tourism industry. North and South Carolina were named for Charles I of England. South Carolina used to rely on its farms for its economy; now forestry is

important, and manufacturing is the most profitable part of the economy.
    We will write again soon.

love,
Donovan and Daisy

State Capital: Columbia, South Carolina
State Capital: Raleigh, North Carolina

They zigzagged through Durham
to find Kitty Hawk,
and decided to fly rather than walk.
Learning a lesson from the brothers named Wright,
they hopped on a plane, and took to flight.

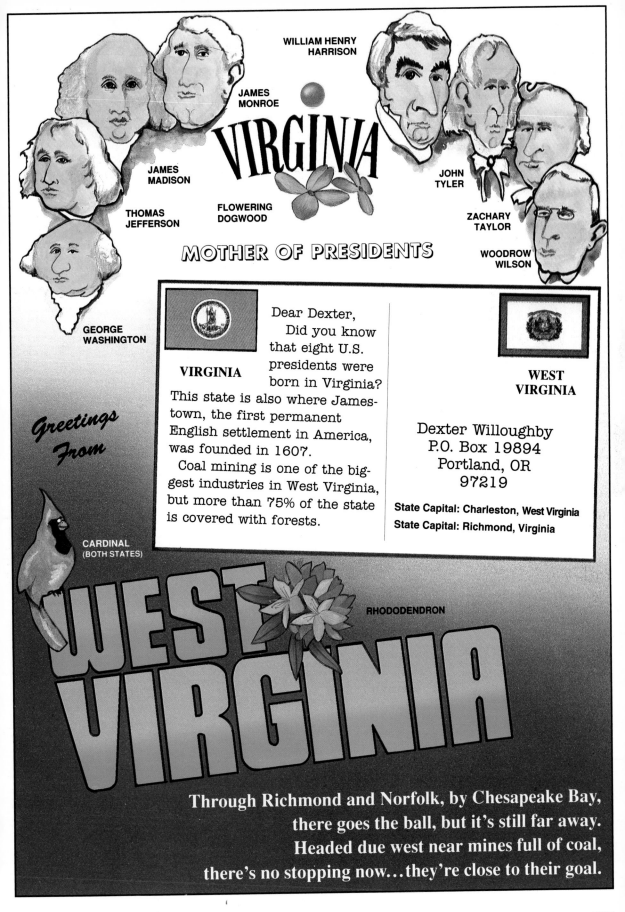

WILLIAM HENRY HARRISON

JAMES MONROE

VIRGINIA

JAMES MADISON

THOMAS JEFFERSON

FLOWERING DOGWOOD

JOHN TYLER

ZACHARY TAYLOR

MOTHER OF PRESIDENTS

WOODROW WILSON

GEORGE WASHINGTON

Greetings From

CARDINAL (BOTH STATES)

VIRGINIA

Dear Dexter,
    Did you know that eight U.S. presidents were born in Virginia? This state is also where Jamestown, the first permanent English settlement in America, was founded in 1607.
    Coal mining is one of the biggest industries in West Virginia, but more than 75% of the state is covered with forests.

WEST VIRGINIA

Dexter Willoughby
P.O. Box 19894
Portland, OR
97219

State Capital: Charleston, West Virginia
State Capital: Richmond, Virginia

WEST VIRGINIA

RHODODENDRON

Through Richmond and Norfolk, by Chesapeake Bay,
there goes the ball, but it's still far away.
Headed due west near mines full of coal,
there's no stopping now…they're close to their goal.

MARYLAND

ANNAPOLIS ★

BLACK-EYED SUSAN

AMERICAN BEAUTY ROSE

WASHINGTON D.C.

NATION'S CAPITAL

BALTIMORE ORIOLE

WASHINGTON D.C.

MARYLAND

Dear Dexter,
     We just finished visiting Maryland and Washington, D.C. Maryland has one of the largest waterfronts in the country. The fishermen along this bay catch amazing amounts of oysters, crabs, clams, and fish. Washington, D.C. (short for District of Columbia), was named in honor of Christopher Columbus. The nation's capital city is also home to the White House, the Washington Monument, the Lincoln and Jefferson Memorials, government offices, and museums.

love, Donovan

State Capital: Annapolis

The kids had no luck, so they sat and they pouted,
when all of a sudden they jumped up and shouted.
"There it goes! See it bounce by the White House front door?"
It's headed due north…bouncing towards Baltimore.

POST CARD

Dear Dexter,
Delaware became a state on December 7, 1787, the first official state in America. The state is named after the Delaware River and Bay. We learned that the river and bay were named for Sir Thomas West, Lord de la Warr. Delaware's chemical industry makes up the main part of the state's economy.
We will be home before long.

love,
Donovan and Daisy

State Capital: Dover

DELAWARE

GEORGE

PEACH BLOSSOM

THE BALL

BLUE HEN CHICKEN

ICE

Across the Delaware they decided to forge,
sailing in a boat with their brave leader, George.
Washington's the man, standing proud and tall,
doing all he can to help find the ball.

RUFFED GROUSE

LIBERTY BELL

PENNSYLVANIA

MOUNTAIN LAUREL

Dear Dexter,
Catching that ball isn't as easy as we thought! It's now taken us into New Jersey and Pennsylvania. New Jersey is known as the Crossroads of the East because the products from its factories can be shipped to 12 states overnight.
Tourism is also really important to the economy in New Jersey.

Pennsylvania plays a big part in our country's history. The Declaration of Independence was signed in Philadelphia in 1776 and the U.S Constitution was written there in 1787.

POST CARD

love, Donovan

State Capital: Harrisburg, Pennsylvania
State Capital: Trenton, New Jersey

NEW JERSEY

Greetings from

VIOLET

EASTERN GOLDFINCH

**Bouncing off the famous bell, the one that has a crack,
the ball crossed into Jersey, close to Hackensack.**

Greetings from **RHODE ISLAND**

VIOLET

NEWPORT JAZZ FESTIVAL

RHODE ISLAND RED

Dear Dexter,

Connecticut factories produce all kinds of products, from sewing machines to submarines. We visited Hartford, home of the *Courant*. The *Courant*, established in 1764, is the oldest newspaper still being published in America. Rhode Island is the smallest state in America, but it is home to many people and industries. Jewelry manufacturing is an important business.

love,
Donovan and Daisy

State Capital: Providence, Rhode Island
State Capital: Hartford, Connecticut

Greetings from **CONNECTICUT**

ROBIN

MOUNTAIN LAUREL

DEFENDERS MONUMENT

They ran through Rhode Island, they raced at top speed,
with Donovan Willoughby, himself, in the lead.
They thought they were gaining—it was quite a surprise—
when the kids lost the ball in the gray Hartford skies.

Dear Dexter,

We are in one of the largest cities in the world. Dexter, did you know New York City served as the nation's capital for a short while and our first president, George Washington, was inaugurated here in 1789.

New York City is the largest manufacturing center in the United States and is very famous for its fashion industry. The state is also known for its tourism, with places to visit like the Statue of Liberty, the Adirondack Mountains, Niagara Falls, and the U.S. Military Academy at West Point.

Post Card

State Capital: Albany

**The Statue of Liberty provided a view
of Broadway, Madison, and Fifth Avenue.
They looked all about—it didn't take long—
to spot the red ball in the arms of King Kong.**

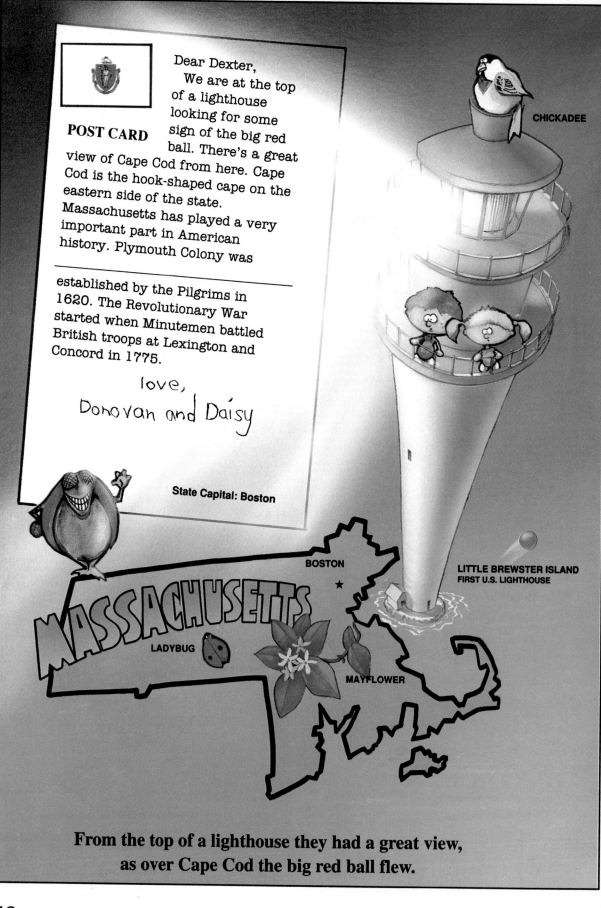

POST CARD

Dear Dexter,
We are at the top of a lighthouse looking for some sign of the big red ball. There's a great view of Cape Cod from here. Cape Cod is the hook-shaped cape on the eastern side of the state. Massachusetts has played a very important part in American history. Plymouth Colony was

established by the Pilgrims in 1620. The Revolutionary War started when Minutemen battled British troops at Lexington and Concord in 1775.

love,
Donovan and Daisy

State Capital: Boston

CHICKADEE

LITTLE BREWSTER ISLAND
FIRST U.S. LIGHTHOUSE

BOSTON

MASSACHUSETTS

LADYBUG

MAYFLOWER

**From the top of a lighthouse they had a great view,
as over Cape Cod the big red ball flew.**

Dear Dexter,

Greetings from Vermont and New Hampshire! The ball sure is giving us a run for our money.

Of the original 13 colonies, New Hampshire was the first to declare independence from Great Britain. Though Vermont was not one of the original 13, it became the first state after them to join the Union. Maple syrup is one of Vermont's most famous products.

We'll be home as soon as we get some skiing done and we catch that red ball!

love, Donovan

NEW HAMPSHIRE

State Capital: Montpelier, Vermont
State Capital: Concord, New Hampshire

Greetings from VERMONT and NEW HAMPSHIRE

RED CLOVER

PURPLE FINCH

HERMIT THRUSH

PURPLE LILAC

**Brilliant colors glowed overhead, from leaves of yellow, orange, and red.
The kids ran by a syrup tree, and headed for the bright blue sea.**

CHICKADEE

WHITE PINE
CONE
& TASSEL

Dear Dexter,
     Here we are in Maine.
Maine is a pretty state that
has become a very popular
vacation spot. Tourists come to
see scenic beaches, lakes,
rivers, and mountains.
You'll love this Dexter! Maine
provides the world with 100
million flat tins of sardines,
and most of the nation's
lobsters come
from Maine's
coast. We're
going fishing.
Donovan

POST CARD

Dexter Willoughby
P.O. Box 19894
Portland, OR
97219

State Capital: Augusta

MAINE

While chatting with a lobster and sitting on a pier,
at last they saw the big red ball, bouncing very near.
Bouncing high and bouncing hard, along the Portland sands,
up it went for one last time and dropped in Daisy's hands.

44

Now back at home, on a beautiful day,
the kids grabbed the ball and went out to play.
But Daisy threw it too fast and too high.
It sailed over Donovan, up into the sky.
Uh oh…

State Facts

ALABAMA p. 31
CAPITAL: Montgomery
NICKNAME: Heart of Dixie
STATEHOOD: Dec. 14, 1819 (22)
STATE DANCE: Square dance

ALASKA p. 9
CAPITAL: Juneau
NICKNAME: The Last Frontier
STATEHOOD: Jan. 3, 1959 (49)
STATE FOSSIL: Woolly mammoth

ARIZONA p. 14
CAPITAL: Phoenix
NICKNAME: Grand Canyon State
STATEHOOD: Feb. 14, 1912 (48)
STATE REPTILE: Arizona ridgenose rattlesnake

ARKANSAS p. 24
CAPITAL: Little Rock
NICKNAME: Land of Opportunity
STATEHOOD: June 15, 1836 (25)
STATE INSECT: Honeybee

CALIFORNIA pp. 10-11
CAPITAL: Sacramento
NICKNAME: Golden State
STATEHOOD: Sept. 9, 1850 (31)
STATE ANIMAL: California grizzly bear

COLORADO p. 16
CAPITAL: Denver
NICKNAME: Centennial State
STATEHOOD: Aug. 1, 1876 (38)
STATE FOSSIL: Stegosaurus

CONNECTICUT p. 39
CAPITAL: Hartford
NICKNAME: Nutmeg State
STATEHOOD: Jan. 9, 1788 (5)
STATE SONG: "Yankee Doodle"

DELAWARE p. 37
CAPITAL: Dover
NICKNAMES: Diamond State; First State
STATEHOOD: Dec. 7, 1787 (1)
STATE INSECT: Ladybug

FLORIDA p. 33
CAPITAL: Tallahassee
NICKNAME: Sunshine State
STATEHOOD: March 3, 1845 (27)
STATE SONG: "Suwannee River"

GEORGIA p. 33
CAPITAL: Atlanta
NICKNAME: Peach State
STATEHOOD: Jan. 2, 1788 (4)
STATE SONG: "Georgia on My Mind"

HAWAII p. 12
CAPITAL: Honolulu
NICKNAME: Aloha State
STATEHOOD: Aug. 21, 1959 (50)
STATE TREE: Kukui (Candlenut)

IDAHO p. 7
CAPITAL: Boise
NICKNAMES: Gem State; Spud State
STATEHOOD: July 3, 1890 (43)
STATE HORSE: Appaloosa

ILLINOIS p. 28
CAPITAL: Springfield
NICKNAME: Prairie State
STATEHOOD: Dec. 3, 1818 (21)
STATE FISH: Bluegill

INDIANA p. 28
CAPITAL: Indianapolis
NICKNAME: Hoosier State
STATEHOOD: Dec. 11, 1816 (19)
STATE TREE: Tulip tree

IOWA p. 26
CAPITAL: Des Moines
NICKNAME: Hawkeye State
STATEHOOD: Dec. 28, 1846 (29)
STATE SONG: "Song of Iowa"

KANSAS p.19
CAPITAL: Topeka
NICKNAME: Sunflower State
STATEHOOD: Jan. 29, 1861 (34)
STATE SONG: "Home on the Range"

KENTUCKY p. 30
CAPITAL: Frankfort
NICKNAME: Bluegrass State
STATEHOOD: June 1, 1792 (15)
STATE TREE: Coffee tree

LOUISIANA p. 24
CAPITAL: Baton Rouge
NICKNAMES: Pelican State; Creole State
STATEHOOD: April 30, 1812 (18)
STATE SONG: "Give Me Louisiana"

MAINE p. 44
CAPITAL: Augusta
NICKNAME: Pine Tree State
STATEHOOD: March 15, 1820 (23)
STATE FISH: Landlocked salmon

MARYLAND p. 36
CAPITAL: Annapolis
NICKNAMES: Free State; Old Line State
STATEHOOD: April 28, 1788 (7)
STATE CRUSTACEAN: Maryland blue crab

MASSACHUSETTS p. 42
CAPITAL: Boston
NICKNAMES: Bay State; Old Colony
STATEHOOD: Feb. 6, 1788 (6)
STATE BEVERAGE: Cranberry juice

MICHIGAN p. 29
CAPITAL: Lansing
NICKNAME: Wolverine State
STATEHOOD: Jan. 26, 1837 (26)
STATE STONE: Petosky stone

MINNESOTA p. 27
CAPITAL: St. Paul
NICKNAMES: North Star State; Land of 10,000 Lakes
STATEHOOD: May 11, 1858 (32)
STATE MUSHROOM: Morel

MISSISSIPPI p. 32
CAPITAL: Jackson
NICKNAME: Magnolia State
STATEHOOD: Dec. 10, 1817 (20)
STATE WATER MAMMAL: Bottle-nosed dolphin

MISSOURI p. 25
CAPITAL: Jefferson City
NICKNAME: Show Me State
STATEHOOD: Aug. 10, 1821 (24)
STATE MUSICAL INSTRUMENT: Fiddle

MONTANA p. 17
CAPITAL: Helena
NICKNAME: Treasure State
STATEHOOD: Nov. 8, 1889 (41)
STATE STONES: Sapphire and agate

NEBRASKA p. 18
CAPITAL: Lincoln
NICKNAME: Cornhusker State
STATEHOOD: March 1, 1867 (37)
STATE ANIMAL: White-tailed deer

NEVADA p. 13
CAPITAL: Carson City
NICKNAMES: Sagebrush State; Silver State
STATEHOOD: Oct. 31, 1864 (36)
STATE GRASS: Indian ricegrass

NEW HAMPSHIRE p. 43
CAPITAL: Concord
NICKNAME: Granite State
STATEHOOD: June 21, 1788 (9)
STATE TREE: White birch

NEW JERSEY p. 38
CAPITAL: Trenton
NICKNAME: Garden State
STATEHOOD: Dec. 18, 1787 (3)
STATE ANIMAL: Horse

NEW MEXICO p. 15
CAPITAL: Santa Fe
NICKNAME: Land of Enchantment
STATEHOOD: Jan. 6, 1912 (47)
STATE INSECT: Tarantula hawk wasp

NEW YORK pp. 40–41
CAPITAL: Albany
NICKNAME: Empire State
STATEHOOD: July 26, 1788 (11)
STATE INSECT: Ladybug

NORTH CAROLINA p. 34
CAPITAL: Raleigh
NICKNAME: Tar Heel State
STATEHOOD: Nov. 21, 1789 (12)
STATE BEVERAGE: Milk

NORTH DAKOTA p. 20
CAPITAL: Bismarck
NICKNAMES: Sioux State; Peace Garden State
STATEHOOD: Nov. 2, 1889 (39)
STATE SONG: "North Dakota Hymn"

OHIO p. 29
CAPITAL: Columbus
NICKNAME: Buckeye State
STATEHOOD: March 1, 1803 (17)
STATE DRINK: Tomato juice

OKLAHOMA p. 21
CAPITAL: Oklahoma City
NICKNAME: Sooner State
STATEHOOD: Nov. 16, 1907 (46)
STATE FLOWER: Mistletoe

OREGON p. 6
CAPITAL: Salem
NICKNAME: Beaver State
STATHOOD: Feb. 14, 1859 (33)
STATE ANIMAL: Beaver

PENNSYLVANIA p. 38
CAPITAL: Harrisburg
NICKNAME: Keystone State
STATEHOOD: Dec. 12, 1787 (2)
STATE DOG: Great Dane

RHODE ISLAND p. 39
CAPITAL: Providence
NICKNAME: Ocean State
STATEHOOD: May 29, 1790 (13)
STATE TREE: Red maple

SOUTH CAROLINA p. 34
CAPITAL: Columbia
NICKNAME: Palmetto State
STATEHOOD: May 23, 1788 (8)
STATE TREE: Palmetto tree

SOUTH DAKOTA p. 20
CAPITAL: Pierre
NICKNAMES: Sunshine State; Coyote State
STATEHOOD: Nov. 2, 1889 (40)
STATE ANIMAL: Coyote

TENNESSEE p. 31
CAPITAL: Nashville
NICKNAME: Volunteer State
STATEHOOD: June 1, 1796 (16)
STATE HORSE: Tennessee walking horse

TEXAS pp. 22–23
CAPITAL: Austin
NICKNAME: Lone Star State
STATEHOOD: Dec. 29, 1845 (28)
STATE FISH: Guadalupe bass

UTAH p. 13
CAPITAL: Salt Lake City
NICKNAME: Beehive State
STATEHOOD: Jan. 4, 1896 (45)
STATE EMBLEM: Beehive

VERMONT p. 43
CAPITAL: Montpelier
NICKNAME: Green Mountain State
STATEHOOD: March 4, 1791 (14)
STATE TREE: Sugar maple

VIRGINIA p. 35
CAPITAL: Richmond
NICKNAMES: The Old Dominion; Mother of Presidents
STATEHOOD: June 25, 1788 (10)
STATE SHELL: Oyster shell

WASHINGTON p. 8
CAPITAL: Olympia
NICKNAMES: Evergreen State; Chinook State
STATEHOOD: Nov. 11, 1889 (42)
STATE FISH: Steelhead trout

WEST VIRGINIA p. 35
CAPITAL: Charleston
NICKNAME: Mountain State
STATEHOOD: June 20, 1863 (35)
STATE ANIMAL: Black bear

WISCONSIN p. 27
CAPITAL: Madison
NICKNAME: Badger State
STATEHOOD: May 29, 1848 (30)
STATE DOMESTIC ANIMAL: Dairy cow

WYOMING p. 17
CAPITAL: Cheyenne
NICKNAME: Equality State
STATEHOOD: July 10, 1890 (44)
STATE GEMSTONE: Jade

About the Authors

Ray Nelson loves to travel. He has traveled to four whole states: Oregon, Washington, California, and Canada! While on his extensive travels he picked up a small fuzzy hitchhiker named Douglas Kelly.

Today Ray and Doug write and illustrate children's books in Portland, Oregon. Ray has a luxurious mansion while Doug lives in a small fig tree in Ray's front yard. Ray loves to play basketball, eat twinkies, and spend time with his wife, Theresa, and their daughter, Alexandria. Doug likes to spend time with Victoria and Toonces, play golf, and eat figs.

Ray and Doug hope someday to travel to exotic places like Des Moines and Peoria.

Special Thanks
Janet Lockwood, Kelly Kuntz, Mike and Holly McLane, Julie Mohr, Ben Adams, Chris Nelson, Michelle Roehm, Jerry Sayer, Joseph Siegel, and Deborah Beilman